PAUL MULDOON was born in 1951 in County Armagh, Northern Ireland. From 1973 to 1986 he worked in Belfast as a radio and television producer for the BBC. Since 1987 he has lived in the USA, where he is now Howard G. B. Clark '21 Professor at Princeton University. Between 1999 and 2004 he was Professor of Poetry at the University of Oxford. Muldoon's most recent collections of poetry are *Medley for Morin Khur* (2005), *Horse Latitudes* (2006), *Plan B* (2009) and *Maggot* (2010). A Fellow of the Royal Society of Literature and the American Academy of Arts and Sciences, Muldoon was elected a Member of the American Academy of Arts and Letters in 2008. Among his awards are the T. S. Eliot Prize, the *Irish Times* Poetry Prize, the Pulitzer Prize for Poetry, the International Griffin Prize, the 2004 American Ireland Fund Literary Award, and the Shakespeare Prize.

ENITHARMON PRESS

First published in 2012
by Enitharmon Press
26B Caversham Road
London NW5 2DU

www.enitharmon.co.uk

Distributed in the UK by
Central Books
99 Wallis Road
London E9 5LN

ISBN: 978-1-907587-25-2

Enitharmon Press gratefully acknowledges the financial support of
Arts Council England through Grants for the Arts.

British Library Cataloguing-in-Publication Data.
A catalogue record for this book is available
from the British Library.

Designed in Albertina by Libanus Press
and printed in England by
Antony Rowe Ltd

CONTENTS

RESISTANCE

Until break of day
It was touch and go
But Juliet gave way
To Romeo
A leader in her field
A Cold War strategist
Isolde would yield
To Tristan's tryst

Your grandmother was in the Resistance
The Gestapo asking questions
The SS at the door
Now we've gone underground
You may have found
You can't resist me much more

In a purple tent
On the Zuider Zee
Cleopatra would relent
To Antony
Once just good friends
In the green wood
Marian would bend
For Robin Hood

Your grandmother was in the Resistance
The Gestapo asking questions
The SS at the door
Now we've gone underground
You may have found
You can't resist me much more

These seventeen miles
Of corridors
Under the Pentagon
I thought I saw you smile
At the perimeter guard
His I.D. read Von Braun

Those seventeen miles
Of corridors
Under the Pentagon
If we spend a while
In close quarters
Maybe you'll fall upon

Your knee and kiss the rod
As the goddess of the chase
Might submit to a Greek god
With a good grace
Or having told her beads
In the convent yard
Heloise would cede
To Abelard

Your grandmother was in the Resistance
The Gestapo asking questions
The SS at the door
Now we've gone underground
You may have found
You can't resist me much more

TILL I MET YOU

Till I met you
I was a flag without a pole
A scrawl without a scroll
A soloist without a cue
A gadfly-sting without a herd
A thing without a word
Till I met you

Till I met you
I was a bird without a perch
A larch without a lurch
A merchantman without a crew
A butterfly without a jar
A sky without a star
Till I met you

There was a sense of something unfulfilled
When I decided to leave
As if we both still
Desperately wanted to believe

Till I met you
I was a scar without a scab
A jape without a jab
A labyrinth without a clew
A bellyful without a bag
A bull without a rag
Till I met you

IF ANY OF THIS GETS OUT

The night in Shepherd's Bush
I crept up on a thrush
And fed it to the cat
You offered Annie
Five quid to see her fanny
In the granny flat
Now I fear some chinwagger
May think because I stagger
I'm a lager lout
There'll be hell to pay
On judgment day
If any of this gets out

The night in Golders Green
I'd fold a fog machine
Into the baby's cot
You were seeing double
As you picked through the rubble
In this latest trouble spot
I was on a sticky wicket
When I crossed the picket
With the ticket tout
But I'll be up shit creek
If there's a press leak
And any of this gets out

The aftershow in Hampstead
With the haulage heiress
Who was such a drag
Though her pass had promised
Access all areas
She resnapped her handbag

She said I trapped this crocodile
With Caproni's goat
During the recent drought
She said look for me in Foxes Dale
In a cement overcoat
If any of this gets out

The night in Kentish Town
I went out in Annie's gown
For another bet
You all but pulled the trigger
On the shady figure
Smoking a cigarette
Now I'm thinking
We must both be stinking
After our absinthe drinking bout
If someone catches a whiff
We'll be in serious diffs
If any of this gets out

PIP AND MAGWITCH

In an effort to distract his victim and throw the police off his scent,
Anwar al-Awlaki had left a paperback of *Great Expectations*
all bundled up with a printer-cartridge bomb. They found his fingerprints
on the page – wouldn't you know? – where Dickens,
having put us all in a quandary on the great marshes of Kent,
now sets us down with Pip and the leg-ironed convict, Abel Magwitch,
Pip forever chained to Magwitch by dint
of having brought him a pork pie and file in a little care-package.

For the moment, he's a seven-year-old whose Christmas Eve's spent
trying to come up with a way to outfox
this hard-line neighbour, unshaven, the smell of a Polo Mint
not quite masking his breath, his cigar twirling in its unopened sarcophagus
like an Egyptian mummy, one dismissive of the chance
it will ever come into its inheritance.

MAD FOR YOU

Looks like King George III
Was out of his gourd
For most of his reign
Had he left the Bronx for Yonkers
Poe would still have gone bonkers
He was so soft in the brain

The author of 'The Raven'
Was completely cuckoo
I may seem unhinged and unshaven
But I'm only mad for you

Looks like Hieronymus Bosch
Talked a lot of tosh
While going round the bend
As for that ersatz Erik Satie
He went completely batty
And jumped off the deep end

The maestro lost his marbles
In *La Maison du Fou*
I may seem gaga and garbled
But I'm only mad for you

I wasn't the cabin boy
On the *Golden Vanity*
Or the naval viceroy
Who voiced that inanity
And as for my misdeeds
With the mermaid (or manatee)
I'm still tempted to plead
Temporary insanity

For it looks like Van Gogh
Still had a one-man show
Despite missing a slate
Though Lear had fallen off his trolley
He'd still fulminate on folly
With his fellow inmates

My top floor is unrented
I may have lost a screw
I may seem deranged and demented
But I'm only mad for you

THIS LAST GREAT COUNTRY SONG

I took the interstate in a '53 V-8
I followed her from Haight
Ashbury to Ashbury Park
And my spirit soared
With that coast-to-coast billboard
Now I get my kicks
When mail-order mavericks
Fill the billboard charts

But my heart still aches
When I think of the kiss
Into which we rushed headlong
I don't know if I can take
Much more of this
This last great country song

I danced a jig at The Blind Pig
I took another swig
From a fifth of Maker's Mark
I walked the buzzard-buzzy sky
Where the deer were getting high
Now I'm on the floor
At the convenience store
Loading soda into a cart

But my heart still quakes
When I reminisce
On drinking all night long
I don't know if I can take
Much more of this
This last great country song

With its failed crops its foreclosed loans
Its store-bought whiskey its wit home-grown
Its waitresses who've left no traces
Of their pantie-lines their X-tans
Their monster-trucking exes their dash-mounted fans
Their fanned-out cartridge cases

Through which I ran for my life from a guy with a knife
I'd been led by his wife
To their trailer park
Where the strung-out utility poles
Still found no use for our lost souls
Now I'll be running for mayor
I'll be leading a prayer
Breakfast next to Wal-Mart

But my heart still breaks
To think I'll no longer be remiss
To think I'll no longer do wrong
I don't know if I can take
Much more of this
This last great country song

IT WON'T BE ANYTIME SOON

I need a man with enough sagacity
To wear a coonskin cap
And escort me and my party
Through the Cumberland Gap
A man sufficiently rough hewn
Not to see shooting a raccoon
As serious crime
You need a man with enough powder and ball
To see that what lies behind a waterfall's
The American sublime
Though you may one day track down your Daniel Boone
It won't be anytime soon

I need a man with just enough gravity
To see how a dripping tap
Will bend the back of a levee
Until you hear it snap
A man sufficiently immune
To the broad strokes of the *Times-Picayune*
As might turn on a dime
You need a man with enough native wit to call
It like it is from the flood wall
Even as the waters climb
Though he may rise one day with the harvest moon
It won't be anytime soon

I need a man with enough lucidity
To read a contour map
Of Zion or Monument Valley
Without the appropriate app
A man sufficiently attuned

To looking beyond buttes and dunes
Of sandstone and shale and lime
You need a man with enough old-fashioned gall
To tell you you look small
In geological time
Though that may one day strike you as opportune
It won't be anytime soon

A DENT

In memory of Michael Allen

The height of one stall at odds with the next in your grandfather's byre
where cattle allowed themselves to speak only at Yule
gave but little sense of why you taught us to admire
the capacity of a three-legged stool

to take pretty much everything in its stride,
even the card-carrying Crow who let out a war-whoop
now your red pencil was poised above my calf-hide
manuscript like a graip above a groop.

The depth of a dent in the flank of your grandfather's cow
from his having leaned his brow
against it morning and night

for twenty years of milking by hand
gave but little sense of how distant is the land
on which you had us set our sights.

LE FLANNEUR

A spirit grocer is still ordained
after seven years ordinarily.
The Flower of Sweet Strabane is still an also-ran
in Tim Humphreys' of Ranelagh.

For as long as curates have gone to the Curragh
their activities have been extracurricular.
It was never a pint of plain in a jug
had the plain people of Ireland by the jugular.

Now the girl on whom you used to dote
is in her dotage.
The *Evening Herald* is less than heraldic.

Though your flesh may not at first look gross
in the window of a spirit grocer's
you can still rely on Myles for a reality check.

3-CAR GARAGE

We got the Camry on the road
My old lady and I
I thought I'd asked her to download
Spirit in the Sky
We were feeling kinda flaccid
When we hit 202
We dropped some amino acid
Like ancient hippies do
By the time we got to Woodstock
It was time for a massage
It may be garage rock
But it's a 3-car garage

I guess she's taken out a loan
From Merrill Lynch or Lloyds
To catch up with the Rolling Stones
And Roger's Pink Floyd
Now you'll find me drinking lattes
In Giants Stadium
And inflating the old lady
To relieve the tedium
They come as less and less a shock
Roger and his pig-barrage
It may be garage rock
But it's a 3-car garage

3-car garages where some little effer
Took out your Lincoln Zephyr
And gave it its first ding
3-car garages where our wives
Caught us thinking our lives
Might be knockoffs of the real thing

But overlook such episodes
Having themselves done stints
In knockoffs of Zandra Rhodes
And Laura Ashley prints
Now they're fitting out their hubbies
With basses in their basements
While all the ancient hippies
Are having hip-replacements
Now we've given up hooch and hock
For Château Lynch-Bages
It may be garage rock
But it's a 3-car garage

CHANCES ARE

What are the chances, would you say,
Carl Sandburg worked on the screenplay
Of *The Greatest Story Ever Told?*
What are the odds
Of Nelson poor sod
Inspiring a wrestling hold?
Chances are flimsy
Cary Grant might suddenly have caught a whimsy
And dropped some LSD
Chances are small
You're a drug they might recall from me

What are the chances, do you think,
The Staten Island ferry would ever sink
With a Vanderbilt at the wheel?
What are the odds
Of the *SS Nimrod*
Being used to hunt harp seals?
Chances are fragile
Shackleton himself is sufficiently agile
To cross your frozen sea
Chances are faint
You'll lodge a lover's complaint with me

About your cousin from Rhinecliff
They talked down from the Rip Van Winkle
Who told me a worm has five hearts
But you've not shown any heart so far
About your cousin from Rhinecliff
Who was so uptight her skirt would wrinkle
She told me a snail shoots its little chalky darts
And takes whatever the chances are

For what are the chances, would you guess,
That the USSR and the US
Would end up in the same bed?
What are the odds
Of an Ichabod
Crane being buried in Bull's Head?
Chances are slender
You'll ever give up on that repeat offender
You met at F.I.T.
Chances are slim
You'd consider leaving him for me

GOOD AS IT GETS

Like Holden Caulfield spotting phonies
Or Stephen Sondheim winning Tonys
You're a sort of pioneer
Like Davy Crockett knowing trails
Or Salome throwing veils
Over what had been quite clear

Though you've not set out
To assuage my doubt
It was obvious from the outset
You're just about as good as it gets

Like Piggy now his glasses were broken
Or Ole Blue Eyes back in Hoboken
With the local racketeers
Like Al Capone in redeeming rum
Or Marilyn in seeming dumb
You're improving with the years

Though you don't quite chime
With my sense of time
And your diary's not a Letts
You're just about as good as it gets

I fell in love with you on the courts
When you showed me your forehand shot
When I teased you about contact sports
And you gave just as good as you got

Like Hans Anderson in *The Ugly Duckling*
Or Errol Flynn in his swashbuckling
And swinging from chandeliers
Like Robin Hood in righting wrongs
Or Ira Gershwin in writing songs
You're pretty much without peer

Though you still don't rub
Shoulders with me at the club
And you're not listed in Debrett's
You're still just about as good as it gets

SHOOT 'EM UP

I don't suppose a bandit often achieves his goal
of swapping a bed-roll for lath and plaster.
Many's a storefront has caved in. Crumpled like a blouse.
Rarely is a mainstay made manifest.

That's why I check out each and every gopher hole
for the mink stole that eluded J. J. Astor.
The varmints back in the boarding house?
They, too, wanted to pin a star on my chest.

I don't suppose a piano is ever quite in tune.
That's why a piano-player will precipitously change course.
We like to think all bottles are made of sugar-glass.

Same with the windows of the saloon.
That's why bandits keep barging in two-to-a-horse.
That's why we have to keep heading 'em off at the pass.

YOU GOT THE ROLEX (I GOT THE ROLODEX)

When Jane and I had a little fling
I thought you'd disregard the whole thing
For your approval seemed tacit
It put us on course
For a nasty divorce
And somehow I
Was feeling hard done by
When we divided our assets
For not only had our marriage been wrecked
But you got the Rolex I got the Rolodex

Though time was clearly not on my side
And I was struggling against the tide
While the world seemed to be your oyster
I'd not drown in brine
Without a lifeline
I wouldn't dwell
In my own little shell
Like a monk shut in his cloister
For I'd been given a way to connect
When you got the Rolex I got the Rolodex

Only this morning one of your doctor gal pals
Set her alarm to slumber
And nuzzled my external auditory canal
And asked how I'd come by her number

That I was able to be in touch
Left her somewhat shocked inasmuch
As she'd thought of herself as unlisted
She'd been reticent
About her dark intent

Till she confessed
She harbored in her breast
The urge to do something twisted
And I mean really twisted
That's why I'm feeling fine in retrospect
That you got the Rolex I got the Rolodex

HEY RACHEL

Hey Rachel
If that's your name
How come the daily special
Is always the same?
Even a lousy anchovy
Can vary its game
An egg over easy
Has something it overcame
Hey Rachel
If that's your name

Hey Rachel
If that's your name
The light under your bushel
Is dying of shame
Even a soda fountain
Can express an aim
An awful pie counter
Can make a counterclaim

Against my plaintive songs of love
Through the diner where you cook
Can't you take off your food-handler's glove
At least while you cock a snook
At my calling out from beyond the soda fountain
At my calling out from behind the mountain?

Hey Rachel
If that's your name
Must you always stand vigil
In the kitchen doorframe?
Even this infernal
Fan can take some blame
A stinking back-burner
Can cherish a flame
Hey Rachel
If that's your name

CONTINUITY GIRL

Let's have no Roman soldiers
Wearing Rolex watches
No gunslingers in Polo
Counting up their notches
No alcoholographic
Star War stormtroopers
Veering right then left in traffic
Let's have no more bleeped-out bloopers
Now you've made everything fit
And follow in the world
Because you've taken note of it
My continuity girl

Let's have no Bengal tigers
On the Russian taiga
No Queen Boudicca
Crash-testing a Quadriga
No gennapoleonic
Officers Perempt-
Orily ordering gins and tonic
One shot full the next shot empty
Now you've made everything fit
And follow in the world
Because you've taken note of it
My continuity girl

Till you failed to reconcile
The credit slip from Duluth
With your claim to be at your mother's side
Down in Lady Lake
And I have you on file
As a twister of the truth

Given just how much pressure you've applied
As you've tried to make
Everything fit
And follow in the world
Because you've taken note of it
My continuity girl

So let's have no Roman soldiers
Wearing Rolex watches
No Jesse Jackson seniors
Grabbing at their crotches
No moghulligatawny
Served as firewater
To the Pawnee or the Shawnee
As they're being led to slaughter
Now you've made everything fit
And follow in the world
Because you've taken note of it
My continuity girl

A GIRAFFE

Though her lorgnette
and evening-gloves
suggest she's made for the role
of an opera-buff
singing along with the score,
her mouth's out of sync
with her own overdub.

A giraffe that flubbed
her lines coming back to drink
just a little more
of the bubbly stuff
from the dried-out mud hole
in which a reflection of
her upper body's already set.

THE ADULT THING

It was obvious Newt and Rudy
Were having an affair
JFK was doing Judy
While Jackie did her hair
Since LBJ and FDR
Opened up the West Wing
The guy at the end of a bar
Has pocketed his ring
And done the adult thing
The adult thing
He's done the adult thing

Since Tarzan cheated with Cheetah
And Monica with Bill
The Master with Margarita
In Margaritaville
Since Prince Charles and Princess Di
Were clearly born to swing
And Henry VIII came to vie
With Martin Luther King
I've done the adult thing
The adult thing
I've done the adult thing

Now I view the world through a salted rim
Since I found out about your night with Jim
And I'm starting to wonder if it's true
Adultery's the adult thing to do

You could see Kobe and Magic
Needed more Triple Sec
While Nelson lay hemorrhagic
On the *Victory*'s deck
At least Einstein would never ask
'How long's a piece of string?'
At least Einstein would never mask
His having had a fling
He did the adult thing
The adult thing
He did the adult thing

PARTY LINES

Back in the day
Before everything was televised
We still found ways
To amuse ourselves
She's a stinking whore
He's a filthy swine
Someone's flinging mud
Someone's tossing slime
That apartment block at 6th and Vine
We'd listen in on party lines

Back in the day
When a quart was two pints
I learned to play
In a pickup band
My first pickup truck
My first traffic fine
When we picked up girls
At the five and dime
Or that discotheque at 6th and Vine
We used the same old party lines

I said, haven't I seen you somewhere before?
She said, I don't go there anymore

Fast forward to the day
Of rain and falling leaves
When she called to say
She'd fallen out of love
Her friends stayed hers
And mine stayed mine
When she and I broke up
Round election time
The oaks and maples at 6th and Vine
Were voting along party lines

SAME OLD SAME OLD

Same thing with Herzog
Plucking from his rucksack
A half-eaten shoe
Same with Archimedes
Still so twee and tweedy
After hitting on the screw

He should have sent some gofer
To buy new pennyloafers
Instead of that same old same old
Same old remold

Same thing with Hendrix
Restrained on the train-tracks
By a single coil
Same with Boccaccio
Dabbing his focaccia
In the midnight oil

Pulling off a hammer on
While writing *The Decameron*
Instead of that same old same old
Same old tenfold

Increase in the divorce rate since the 1960s
Same old thing with inconstancy
Same old fixation on the lack of fixities
Same old thing with you and me

Same thing with Balzac's
Brandy and Triple Sec

And pease porridge hot
Same with the world weary
Dante Alighieri
Looking for the lowest spot

He could have supped zuppa di riso
In *Il Paradiso*
Instead of that same old same old
Pease porridge cold

HONEY

Our plane takes hill upon hill long since cleared of pines. The flash
of matching lakelets. Weather and more weather.
The co-pilot points to at least one benefit
of felling pines for warship-keels, namely how the heather
that pits itself against an old saw-pit
and fills in the great gash
of a logging road also sustains our friends the honeybees.

The coroner at the scene of the crash
found the seams of Buddy Holly's jacket of yellow faux leather
'split almost full-length' and his skull also 'split'.
Buddy's personal effects amounted to a pair of cufflinks together
with the top of a ballpoint pen and, barely within his remit,
the $193.00 in cash
from which the coroner deducted $11.65 in fees.

RECALCULATING

I

Arthritis is to psoriasis as Portugal is to Brazil.
Brazil is to wood as war club is to war.
War is to wealth as performance is to appraisal.
Appraisal is to destiny as urn is to ear.

Ear is to grasshopper as China is to DDT.
Tea is to leaf as journalist is to source.
Source is to leak as Ireland is to debt.
Debt is to honor as arthritis is to psoriasis.

II

Wait. Isn't arthritis to psoriasis as Brazil is to Portugal?
Portugal is to *fado* as Boaz is to Ruth.
Ruth is to cornfield as wave is to particle.

III

Particle is to beach as pebble is to real estate.
Realty is to reality as sky is to earth.
Earth is to all ye know as done is to dusted.

ONE-HIT WONDER

Like Chubby Checker as a twister
The Virginian by Owen Wister
Or *Shane* by Jack Schaeffer
Each a single flare
Hanging in the air
With the Archies' 'Sugar, Sugar'
Like a flash of lightning
Stealing its own thunder
Our love's a one-off thing
We're a one-hit wonder

We've risen above the mediocre
With *Dracula* by Bram Stoker
And *Frankenstein* by Mary Shelley
But we're still resigned
To being in a bind
Like *Catch-22* by Joseph Heller
And *The Unbearable Lightness of Being*
By Milan Kundera
Our love's a one-off thing
We're a one-hit wonder

Once it seemed we were like a song or book
That might for a moment enthrall
Now it seems we're like that same song or book
In being in for the long haul

Like *Journey to the End of the Night* by Celine
Or 'Come On Eileen'
By Dexy's Midnight Runners

Like the call once heard
In Harper Lee's *To Kill a Mockingbird*
Or The Knack's 'My Sharona'
Like Kate Chopin's *The Awakening*
With its sudden glow before it goes under
Our love's a one-off thing
We're a one-hit wonder

THE HILLBILLY HILTON

The motel near the trailer park
Where I-40 does that thing
You know from hollers in the dark
A wedding's in full swing
These men were once strong silent types
Who've got the silent treatment
From women who smoke corncob pipes
Only on grand occasions
This may or may not be a ham
These mustard greens are wilting
Under the weight of candied yams
Up at The Hillbilly Hilton
The Hillbilly Hilton puts the ten in Tennessee
The Hillbilly Hilton has a vacancy
The Hillbilly Hilton welcomes you and me

What they've swept beneath that rug
Is just a dead coonhound
To which someone had passed a jug
Of stuff most cops impound
The sheriff here's 'Cornpone' McKeown
Who also runs room service
He'll feed your grandma grandpa's bones
Because she's epileptic
After your grandma has a chew
It's time for a little quilting
That's what passes for pay-per-view
Up at The Hillbilly Hilton
The Hillbilly Hilton an ax is the master key
The Hillbilly Hilton has a vacancy
The Hillbilly Hilton welcomes you and me

Those stories to which you're alluding
Of families still feuding
Over a property line
And our marrying our cousins
'Cos they're a dime a dozen
Are just so much moonshine

It turns out what we took for ham
Was possum or woodchuck
The bridal bed is a Dodge Ram
With monster tires for luck
A gunrack's standard on the post
In case the going's heavy
The minibar has squirrel brains on toast
To help us through the munchies
Your grandma's having an attack
You know from how she's tilting
The toilet's somewhere way out back
Up at The Hillbilly Hilton
The Hillbilly Hilton helps control incontincency
The Hillbilly Hilton has a vacancy
The Hillbilly Hilton still welcomes you and me

11 O'CLOCK

No time since I was a youth
Falling on my front tooth
And chipping the enamel
No time since my squiggles
Charted dogfights with Biggles
In a Sopwith Camel

All that blood and spit
Now I'd locked
Horns with the Messerschmitt
At 11 o'clock
11 o'clock 11 o'clock
The Messerschmitt at 11 o'clock

No time since I baled out
Over a field of Brussels sprouts
Near the Belgian border
No time since I would injure
My good name with Ginger
When the barmaid called last orders

Would it be lager and lime
Or scotch on the rocks
Now that closing time
Was 11 o'clock
11 o'clock 11 o'clock
Now that closing time was 11 o'clock?

No time since I made the overture
To Ginger and she said sure
Though it's like having to endure
The Germans bombing Hull
Before flying up the Humber

No time from the get-go
To the point in the show
Where she and I know
It only seems like a lull
Before the 11 o'clock number

No time since we boarded the airport bus
Till it's dawned on us
We've flown our final mission
The height of Biggles' adventures
Now losing his dentures
To a case-hardened mortician

Now all we hear at the aerodrome
Is chocks
Away Algie for the funeral home
at 11 o'clock
11 o'clock 11 o'clock
The funeral home at 11 o'clock

FRIENDS OF ENITHARMON

The following have generously become Patrons and Sponsors of the *Friends of Enitharmon* scheme, enabling this and other publications to come into being:

PATRONS

Duncan Forbes
Sean O'Connor
Masatsugu Ohtake
Myra Schneider

SPONSORS

Kathy & Jeff Allinson
Colin Beer
Natasha Curry
Vanessa Davis
Jack Herbert
Alison M. Houston
Sylvia Riley
Angela Sorkin
Janet Upward

Winnie-the-Pooh's

50 things
to do
on
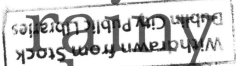

rainy
days

EGMONT

We bring stories to life

First published in Great Britain in 2019 by Egmont UK Limited,
The Yellow Building, 1 Nicholas Road, London W11 4AN

www.egmont.co.uk

Additional decorations by Andrew Grey
Written by Chloë Boyes
Designed by Jeannette O'Toole and Cassie Benjamin

ISBN 978 1 4052 9301 3
70086/001
Printed in Malaysia

Egmont takes its responsibility to the planet and its inhabitants very seriously.
We aim to use papers from well-managed forests run by responsible suppliers.

Adult supervision is recommended when glue, paint, scissors and
other sharp points are in use.

Stay safe online. Egmont is not responsible for content
hosted by third parties.

Acknowledgments

Dreamstime.com

ID 21081557 © Abdulsatarid, p. 31; ID 53182716 © Akinshin, p. 26; ID 111045799 © Alexandr Kornienko, p. 43; ID 28966535 © Alfio Scisetti, p. 26; ID 70025908 © Anna Kucherova, p. 26; ID 40731610 © Anna Kucherova, p. 52; ID 94542230 © Annilein, p. 60; ID 25162966 © Bhofack2, p. 59; ID 35663687 © Brenda Carson, p. 22; ID 86986398, ID 86987217 © Brighton, p. 25; ID 44099476 © Chavarit Opassirivit, p. 14, 43; ID 48814073 © Cherniyvg, p. 47; ID 31151806 © Christoph Weihs, p. 52; ID 52182094 © Delstudio, p. 6, 61; ID 34879869 © Dimitar Marinov, p. 7, 12, 14, 16-17, 30-31, 74; ID 18026710 © Dmitry Ekimovsky, p. 35; ID 19876876 © Dreammasterphotographer, p. 52; ID 22617673 © Dvmsimages, p. 2, 7, 27, 74; ID 7948079 © Ekays, p. 16, 40; ID 35318427 © Embe2006, p. 26; ID 114925616 © Evgeny Prokofyev, p. 51; ID 112976691 © Evgenyatamanenko, p. 34; ID 95037922 © Evgenyatamanenko, p. 65, 79; ID 46372716 © Exopixel, p. 2, 7, 14, 74; ID 86394132 © Famveldman, p. 70-71; ID 99612629 © Famveldman, p. 78; ID 51184881 © Fotyma, p. 3, 70; ID 100232278 © Gabriela Bertolini, p. 25; ID 19034988 © Gaja, p. 64; ID 12366117 © George Burba, p. 51; ID 100289014 © Georgerudy, p. 29; ID 27927920 © Grafner, p. 2, 6, 56-57, 61, 74; ID 76210895 © Ian Andreiev, p. 36; ID 106523601 © John558616, p. 51; ID 10863678 © Joingate, p. 18, 56-57; ID 3314850 © Kasia Biel, p. 62; ID 1524722 © Kati1313, p. 60; ID 108813087 © Keport, p. 55; ID 5909044 © Kheng Ho Toh, p. 60; ID 64162211 © Ksushsh, p. 26; ID 27926020 © Kuzma, p. 52; ID 16878398 © Lana Langlois, p. 55; ID 89636084 © Lenasveica, p. 55; ID 22458544 © Ipb, p. 43; ID 108380431 © Makidotvn, p. 35; ID 39624048 © Marsia16, p. 38-39; ID 37004639 © Melica, p. 24; ID 116852323 © Muhamad Edy Abdul Kasim, p. 32-33; ID 56157877, ID 59845647, ID 85479587 © Nikmerkulov, p.55; ID 93240562 © Nunthana Setila, p. 37; ID 31604723 © Okea, p. 3, 68; ID 110565454 © Oleg Dudko, p. 34; ID 73142222 © Omegaforest, p. 53; ID 87951207, ID 87951636, ID 87954006 © Photographyfirm, p. 24-25; ID 29662596 © Photographerlondon, p. 47; ID 102918767, ID 102919085 © Pichai Pipatkuldilok, p. 51; ID 64997868 © Pixelrobot, p. 17; ID 80635458 © Robert Kneschke, p. 46; ID 76598287 © Romrodinka, p. 52; ID 77339206 © Ruslanchik, p. 26, 55; ID 5243667 © Ryan Pike, p. 59; ID 72938512 © Sergey Novikov, p. 30-31; ID 34659610 © Sergey Novikov, p. 33; ID 72936267 © Sergey Novikov, p. 40; ID 65827970 © Shurinberg, p. 53; ID 100597237 © Sian Cox, p. 6, 61; ID 87806531 © Smileus, p. 55; ID 18976823 © Sonechka, p. 62; ID 27294824 © Stephen Denness, p. 23; ID 88887046 © Stockcreations, p. 60; ID 90379815 © Tatyana Tomsickova, p. 40; ID 109002134 © Tatyana Vychegzhanina, p. 53; ID 105383451 © Tereeez, p. 26; ID 116246958 © Toxitz, p. 52; ID 24966221 © Vadim Yerofeyev, p. 56-57; ID 25557373 © Venusangel, p. 46-47; ID 47101595 © Vetkit, p. 46-47; ID 38053547 © Volkop, p. 3, 56; ID 24427372 © Woraphon Banchobdl, p. 47; ID 50301460 © Yuriy Hnatenko, p. 2, 25, 40, 74; ID 13397548 © Zoom-zoom, p. 50-51

Shutterstock.com

Africa Studio, p. 22; Denis Kuvaev, p. 62; Dmytro Zinkevych, p. 48; sirtravelalot, p. 52

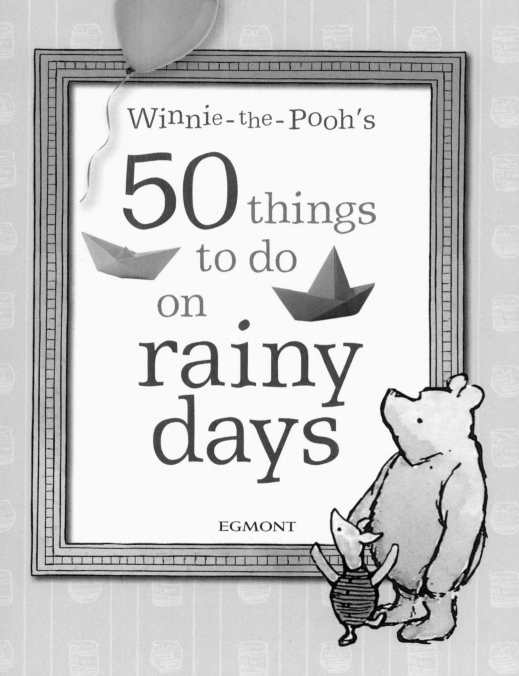

Winnie-the-Pooh's

50 things
to do
on
rainy
days

EGMONT

Health and safety

Adult supervision will be required for a number of the activities described in this book. Where relevant, the activity will be flagged at the top of the page and within the activity.

Adult supervision is recommended when glue, paint, scissors and other sharp points are in use. Wear protective clothing and cover surfaces to avoid staining.

The rainy day adventures

of

....

....

Contents

Tick ✔ each task when completed.

Fun and games

Wherever they go, and whatever happens to them on the way, in that enchanted place on the top of the Forest a little boy and his Bear will always be playing.

① Owl says

This game is best with three or more players. Cut out the character cards on page 75.

Whoever is playing Owl shows one card at a time to the group whilst saying: "Owl says, act like ..." Players must do their best to act like the character on the card.

However, sometimes Owl may show a card and say "Act like ..." without the "Owl says". If this happens, players should stay still. Anyone who moves is out! The last player left is the winner.

2 Race raindrops

These are my two drops of rain
Waiting on the window-pane.
I am waiting here to see
Which the winning one will be.

Use sticky tape to make start and finish lines. Then choose your raindrops and follow their journey. You could pretend to be a sports presenter and commentate on the race.

11

3 Woozles and Wizzles

Fold a piece of paper into four. The first person draws the head at the top of the page. Then fold the paper over to hide the head and pass it to a friend to draw the upper body. Keep going in the same way, adding legs and feet.

Unravel the paper and take a look at the strange character you've created together! Have you made a fearsome Woozle? Or perhaps it's a Wizzle?

Pooh

Use the character cards on page 75 to make the game a bit more challenging! Each player can pick a card and draw the head, body or legs of their character when it's their turn.

Eeyore

Rabbit

④ Pin the tail on Eeyore

Draw or print off a picture of Eeyore and a picture of his tail.

Stick Eeyore to a door or wall and add tape or tack to the top of the tail.

Blindfold players one at a time and spin them around so that they can't cheat.

Then hand them the tail and see if they can find where it should go.

You will need an adult's help.

Make sure to guide people if they are walking wearing a blindfold, or there could be accidents.

13

5 Scavenger hunt

Race to find everything on the list as quickly as you can. Tick ✔ each item when you find it.

1 ◯ Hat

2 ◯ Something orange

3 ◯ Book

4 ◯ Something shiny

5 ◯ Photograph

6 ◯ Something older than me

7 ◯ Peppercorns

8 ◯ Something to draw with

9 ◯ Shoelace

10 ◯ Something noisy

6 I spy

You can play this game anywhere – challenge each other to guess what you have spied at home, on the train or in the car.

I spy, with my little eye, something beginning with ...

7 Balloon tennis

See how long you can keep a balloon in the air, whilst batting it to each other. You can use your hands or make a bat out of a rolled up newspaper.

15

Fortune teller

1 Fold a square piece of paper in half to make a triangle. Open it up and refold the other way so that a cross forms in the middle of the square.

2 Fold each of the corners into the middle point.

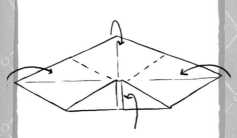

3 Turn the paper over and fold the four corners into the middle this way, too.

4 Turn the paper over again so you can see four small squares. Fold in half each way.

5 Thread your fingers into the squares and pinch each side to form the fortune teller shape.

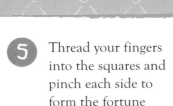

6

Now unfold your fortune teller and add your messages. You could write ideas about things to do on a rainy day, like playing a game from this book or having a little snack of honey! Refold the fortune teller and add coloured dots to the outside and numbers to the inside flaps. Ask a friend to pick a colour and a number and then tell them their fortune!

17

9 Flap the fish

First of all, cut out fish shapes
from an old newspaper. Line the fish up at
the starting line. Then, using a piece of
card as a fan, flap the newspaper fish to make
them move forwards. Race your fish to the
finish line. The first fish over the line
is the winner!

Pooh

Tigger

Piglet

10

Charades

Use the cards on page 75 for this game. Players take it in turns to pick up a card, not showing anyone else. Then, they must act like the character on the card and the other players try to guess who it is.

Eeyore

Roo

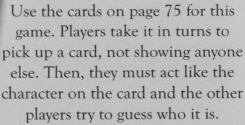

Kanga

Rabbit

Christopher Robin

11 Hide and seek

This game can be played with two or more people. Choose one person to be the seeker. The seeker counts to twenty while everyone else hides. When they have finished counting, they must run to find everyone. The last one found is the winner.

Be imaginative

If I had a ship,
I'd sail my ship,
I'd sail my ship
Through Eastern seas.

12 Sock puppets

Put on your own puppet show with homemade sock puppets.

You will need:

☆ Odd socks
☆ Marker pen
☆ Googly eyes
☆ Wool
☆ Felt

Put a sock on your hand, stretching your fingers to the end and your thumb in the heel.

Use a marker pen, stickers and googly eyes to give your puppet a face. Glue wool on the top for hair and add a felt tongue, if you like.

Why not try making your sock puppet look like Piglet or Tigger?

13 Mosaic art

You will need an adult's help.

You will need:

☆ Coloured paper (old wrap or scrap paper)
☆ Pencil
☆ Scissors
☆ Glue stick
☆ 1 sheet of card

Firstly, cut or tear your coloured paper into small pieces.

Draw your design onto the card in pencil.

Then build up the detail of your picture using the mosaics.

Try using different colours to make patterns.

14 Pom-pom tails

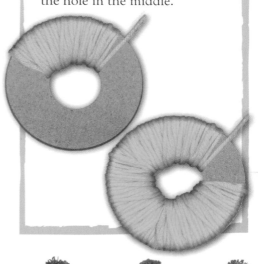

You will need:

☆ Wool
☆ Tumbler or mug
☆ Large button or £2 coin
☆ Scissors
☆ Pencil
☆ Cardboard

Hold the two circles together and thread the wool around the edge. Continue winding the wool around until you can't see any cardboard and you have filled the hole in the middle.

Use a mug to draw two circles on the cardboard. Then draw a smaller circle inside each, using the button/coin as a template. Cut out the smaller circles so you have two doughnut shapes.

3

Carefully snip around the edge, in between the two pieces of cardboard until you've cut all around the circle.

You will need an adult's help.

4

Thread a length of wool around the pom-pom, in between the two pieces of cardboard. Tie very tightly in a knot to secure.

You could stick your pom-poms on a picture of a rabbit to make a fluffy tail or hang them in your room as decorations!

5

Cut the cardboard away from the pom-pom and fan out into a circle. Trim the edges to make it even.

feathers

shells

15 Museum

When it's grey outside, find interesting objects from your room or around the house and put them on display, just like you would see in a museum. Ask people to come and visit. You could show what you've collected on holidays or days out, or just display some of your favourite things.

pebbles

Pooh stick

photo

badges

16 Marble run

You will need:

☆ Toilet roll/kitchen roll tubes
☆ Sticky tape
☆ Scissors
☆ Paper plates

You will need an adult's help.

1. Cut the tubes in half lengthways. You will also need to leave some whole to use as supports.

2. Tape the halved tubes together to make a long chute. Use smaller pieces of the tubes to make corners if you want your chute to change direction.

3. Use paper plates to make a spiral chute. Support the chute with leftover tubes as it slopes.

4. Now add your marbles and watch as they fly through the run!

A flight of stairs can make a marble run even more fun, but always be careful when playing on stairs.

17 Kitchen band

Turn old boxes and recycling into musical instruments.

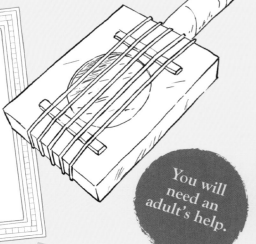

Guitar

Wrap five elastic bands around an old tissue box. Try and find bands that are different in thickness as this will give you high and low notes. Pluck the bands to make your guitar sound.

You will need an adult's help.

Rattle

Cut out two circles of greaseproof paper, about the size of a jam jar lid. Fit one over the end of a toilet roll tube and secure with an elastic band. Add some uncooked rice inside the tube. Then close up the other end using the second piece of greaseproof paper. Shake your rattle up and down to make your sound.

18 Treasure hunt X

First of all, decide what your treasure will be. It could be a favourite toy or book, or a tasty treat! Then hide the treasure somewhere and keep it a secret.

Now draw a map so that you can remember where you've hidden the treasure. Put a big X on the map to mark where the treasure is hidden.

You could give your map to a friend and see if they can find the treasure.

If you want your map to look like a pirate's treasure map, you can rip the edges and stain it with cold tea.

31

19 Paper aeroplanes

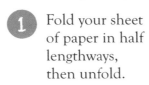

1 Fold your sheet of paper in half lengthways, then unfold.

2 Fold the top two corners so they meet in the middle.

3 Turn the plane over and fold again so that the edges of the top triangle meet in the middle again.

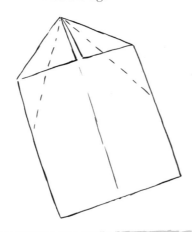

4 Fold the plane in half.

5 Fold the wings down. Repeat on both sides.

Your plane is ready. Now hold a race to see whose travels furthest!

20 Dressing up

Find some old clothes – a hat, feather boa, scarves and sunglasses. Imagine you are on an adventure – you could be an explorer discovering a new kind of animal or a daredevil, about to take part in a brand new stunt.

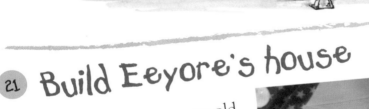

21 Build Eeyore's house

Use sofa cushions or an old sheet draped over chairs as a hideaway. Your den is the perfect place to read or play games with friends - just like Eeyore's house of sticks!

㉒ Home cinema

On small pieces of paper write the name of your film, where the cinema is, what time it will start and the price. Colour in the tickets and give them to your guests.

Close the curtains and grab duvets and blankets so you and your guests feel comfy. Use a torch to show everyone to their seats and bring popcorn to share.

Cinema Ticket
★★★
000728
000728

23 Write a play

Before you start writing, decide what you would like your play to be about.

Some things to think about:

Once you're happy, why not ask some friends if they'd like to perform it with you?

Characters
– how they look and talk, what they wear.

Brave adventures

Setting
– past, present or future?

Exploring

Plot
– will it be funny or sad?

Search for Heffalumps

Day at school

Stage directions
– where to stand, how to say lines.

36

24

Time capsule

Find a tin or plastic box to make a time capsule. Bury it in the garden and dig it up in the future.

Things to include:

☆ Photo of you, friends and family
☆ List of favourite hobbies, music, TV show, film, book, your best friends
☆ Small toys
☆ A drawing
☆ Stickers to decorate your box
☆ Curl of hair
☆ Something you had as a baby

Ask an adult for permission.

25 # Late night feast

Gather your snacks in advance. Make sure you choose quiet food (no crisps, you'll wake everyone!) Late night feasts are perfect for sleepovers with friends.

26 Finger knitting

You will need an adult's help.

Winnie-the-Pooh and Piglet know how important best friends are. Follow the steps to finger knit friendship bracelets for your friends.

1

Create a slipknot and loop it over your index finger.

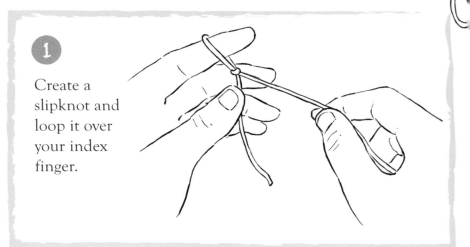

2 Loop the yarn around your finger again, closer to your finger tip than the first loop.

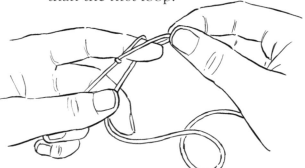

Next, pull the first loop up and over the second and off your finger.

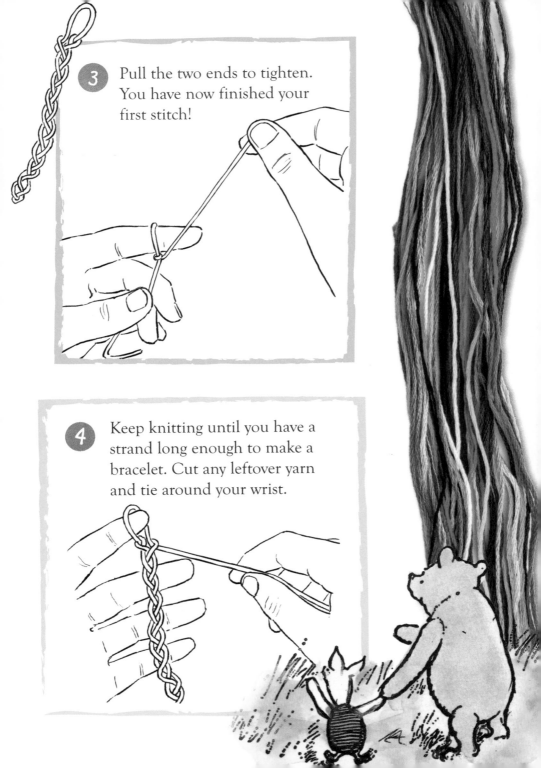

3 Pull the two ends to tighten. You have now finished your first stitch!

4 Keep knitting until you have a strand long enough to make a bracelet. Cut any leftover yarn and tie around your wrist.

27 Build a race car

Old cardboard boxes are perfect for playing with on rainy days.

If your box has high sides, cut holes to make windows.

Use paper plates, coloured paper or felt tip pens to make wheels and a steering wheel.

If you have more than one box, cut out the bottoms and stack them on top of each other. Cut windows and use tin foil to make an enormous space rocket. Now you can travel all the way into space! You might see an alien or a black hole.

Ask an adult for permission.

Keep moving

Christopher Robin goes
Hoppity,
hoppity,
Hoppity,
hoppity,
HOP.

28

The floor is lava

Imagine that the floor of your living room is
made from boiling lava and you must not touch it.
Use the sofas and cushions to make a path
over the lava and escape
the danger!

㉙ Skittles

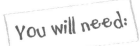

You will need:

☆ Empty plastic bottles
☆ Soft ball

Set your skittles up at the end of a room or hallway. You can add water to make them heavier. Make sure you screw the lid on very tightly!

Take it in turns to roll the ball into the skittles and see how many you can knock over. After each player has thrown, count their score and set the skittles back up for the next player.

The player who knocks the most skittles over after ten rolls each is the winner!

43

30 Gymnastics

Round about, And round about

And round about I go.

Winnie-the-Pooh
is short and stout, but just
look at him doing his exercises!
See if you can do some exercises too.
Can you do a forward roll or
even a handstand?
How long can you hold a
handstand for?
Ask someone to time you.
Make sure you have lots
of space.

You will
need an
adult's help.

㉛ Indoor sports day

Bounce, hop and jump like the friends
of the Hundred Acre Wood. On a rainy
afternoon bring sports day activities inside.

Wiggle your way through hula hoops, jump
over sofa cushions and balance bean bags
on your head to create an obstacle course.

Use pillowcases for a sack race
and ping-pong balls for an
egg and spoon race.

32 Bubbles

There's lots of fun to be had with
a pot of bubbles and a bubble wand.

Try making the biggest bubble you
can, then make lots of tiny ones.

Can you blow a bubble and then
run to follow it as it rises?

Jump up to pop all the bubbles
you have made!

Getting messy

He thought for a moment and said: 'I shall try to look like a **small black cloud.** That will deceive them.' ... [so] Winnie-the-Pooh went to a **very muddy place** that he knew of, and rolled and rolled until he was black all over.

33 Clay play

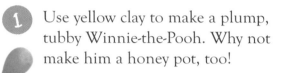

Get creative with squishy, gooey modelling clay and have hours of fun with different colours and shapes.

1 Use yellow clay to make a plump, tubby Winnie-the-Pooh. Why not make him a honey pot, too!

2 You won't need very much clay to make little Piglet! Don't forget his green jumper.

3 If you make a clay Kanga you can have lots of fun bouncing her around the table. Can you make a tiny Roo, too?

34 Smoothies

Mix all of your favourite fruits and vegetables together, with water or yogurt, to make yummy and healthy smoothies.

Bananas and strawberries work well to make sweet smoothies or for something healthier, that Rabbit would enjoy, try a carrot and apple smoothie.

Winnie-the-Pooh would be sure to add honey to his smoothie!

What will you choose?

You will need an adult's help.

52

Pasta play

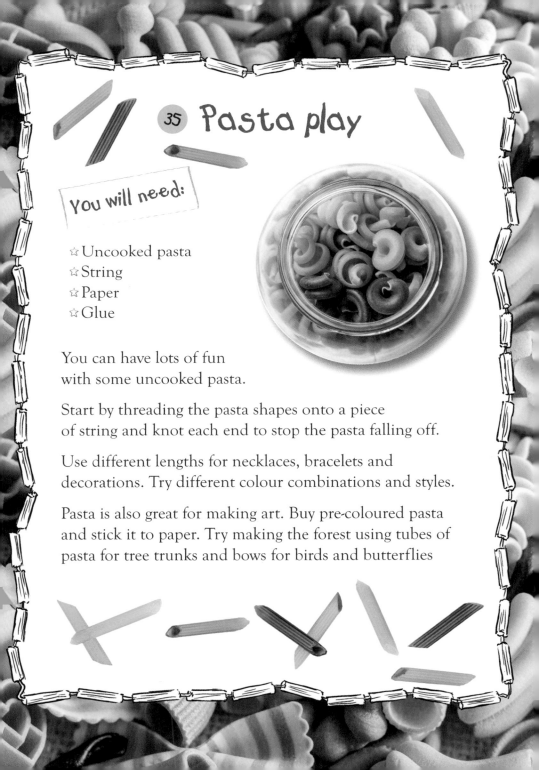

You will need:

☆ Uncooked pasta
☆ String
☆ Paper
☆ Glue

You can have lots of fun with some uncooked pasta.

Start by threading the pasta shapes onto a piece of string and knot each end to stop the pasta falling off.

Use different lengths for necklaces, bracelets and decorations. Try different colour combinations and styles.

Pasta is also great for making art. Buy pre-coloured pasta and stick it to paper. Try making the forest using tubes of pasta for tree trunks and bows for birds and butterflies

36 Floating and sinking

Different objects sink or float in water. Use a washing up bowl or bathtub to test what sinks and what floats.

You will need an adult's help.

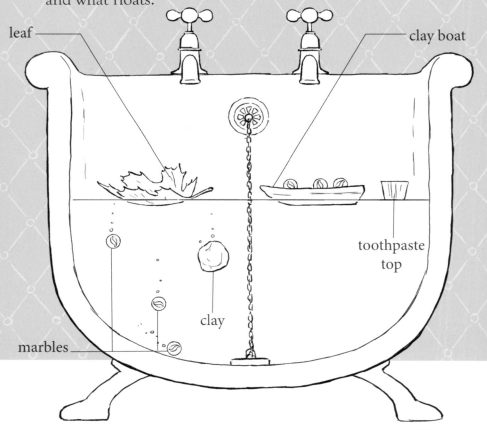

leaf

clay boat

toothpaste top

clay

marbles

On their own, marbles sink, but if you shape modelling clay to make a boat, you can rest the marbles inside and make them float! What else can you find that floats?

37 Shoebox scene

Winnie-the-Pooh and his friends love to explore the Hundred Acre Wood. When you're stuck inside, create your own forest to explore.

Use an old shoebox to hold your mini Hundred Acre Wood. Roll up card to make the trees and collect leaves, twigs and pebbles to add to the floor.

38 Paper mache

Paper mache is a fun way of making masks, hats and crafts. It can get very messy, so put old newspaper down before you begin.

You will need:

☆ 3 cups of flour
☆ 3 cups of water
☆ Balloon
☆ Paintbrush
☆ Newspaper
☆ Masking tape

1 Tear the newspaper into long, thin strips.

2 Add flour and water to a bowl and stir until mixed.

3 Blow up your balloon to the same size as your head.

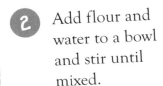

4 Dip the strips of newspaper into your flour/water mix. Once the strips are covered, lay them onto the balloon. Keep adding strips until the whole balloon is covered in several layers.

You will need an adult's help.

5 Leave the balloon to dry overnight. Once it's dry, pop the balloon with a pin and it's ready to paint.

To make a Wise Owl, roll up small bits of newspaper for a beak, claws and eyes. Use masking tape to stick them on. You can cover the tape up when you paint your owl.

39 Honey cupcakes

Winnie-the-Pooh's favourite food is honey. Use this recipe for honey cupcakes to share with your friends.

Ingredients:

- ☆ 115g butter
- ☆ 115g caster sugar
- ☆ 115g self-raising flour
- ☆ 2 eggs
- ☆ 1 tbsp honey

For the icing:
- ☆ 100g icing sugar
- ☆ 50g butter
- ☆ 3 tbsp cold water

Optional:
honeycomb chocolate

You will need an adult's help.

1. Pre-heat the oven to 180°C. Add paper cases to a baking tray.

2. Add all of your cake ingredients to a bowl and stir well.

3. Divide the mixture into the cake cases and put in the oven for 15 minutes.

4. For the icing, beat butter, icing sugar and water together.

5. Once the cakes have finished cooking and have cooled, smooth the icing over the top. If using the honeycomb chocolate, crumble this over the icing.

40

Marshmallow tower

Challenge your friends to make the tallest marshmallow tower they can. Join spaghetti together by pushing the ends into marshmallows and see how tall your tower can be!

41 Homemade ice cream

Impress your friends by making your own ice cream, using just a few ingredients.

You will need:
☆ Milk
☆ Cream
☆ Drinking chocolate
☆ Ice cubes
☆ Salt

1. Mix two spoons of milk, one spoon cream and one spoon drinking chocolate in a bowl.

2. Next, add ice cubes and lots of salt to your bowl and place the glass on top.

3. Surround the glass with more ice cubes and salt.

4. Place a tea towel over the bowl and leave for one hour.

How will you decorate your ice cream? Maybe you can make it look like Pooh or his friends!

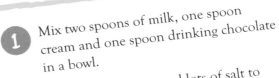

42 Handprint Heffalumps

Use your hands to create monsters and Heffalumps. Put down old newspaper before you start and wear an apron as this can get *very* messy!

Cover your hands with water-based paint. Then press your hand onto your paper, trying not to smudge it.

Lift your hand off and let the paint dry. Use felt tips for antennae, claws and hair and stick on googly eyes.

You could even try the same thing with footprints, just like Winnie-the-Pooh on a muddy day!

43 Paint fun

Have some fun with water-based paint and try different ways of creating patterns.

Use a paintbrush or old toothbrush to flick paint onto a big piece of paper. Try different colours to make a rainbow.

Add a blob of paint to your paper. Use a straw to blow the paint across the page in different directions.

Try these different ways of painting and see which is your favourite. Can you think of any other ways to experiment with paint?

After all that fun you might need a good scrub!

Brave
the rain

"It rained and it rained and it rained.
Piglet told himself that never in all his life,
and he was goodness knows how old – three, was
it, or four? – never had he seen so much rain.
Days and days and days."

44

Search for animals

Some animals love the rain and will come out when it's especially wet.

Look under rocks and plants to search for animals like frogs and beetles.

Dig in the mud to find worms and visit your local pond to see ducks enjoying the rain!

45 Buttercup boats

Find a hill and look for a little stream of water running down. Pick some leaves or flowers and drop them at the top. Watch how they flow down. You could race buttercup boats with a friend.

46 Splash in puddles

Sometimes, when the weather is grey and rainy, the best thing to do is to put on your wellies and run outside. Find puddles to jump over and to splash in and try to dodge the raindrops.

Who can find the biggest, muddiest puddle?

You will need an adult's help.

47 Rain measurer

Every morning he went out with his umbrella and put a stick in the place where the water came up to ... On the morning of the fifth day he saw the water all round him, and knew that for the first time in his life he was on a real island. Which was very exciting.

You will need:

☆ Plastic bottle
☆ Felt tips/marker
☆ Tape measure
☆ Scissors

1 Start by cutting the top section of the bottle.

2 Turn the top upside down and place inside the bottle, to create a funnel.

3 Measure from the bottom of the bottle up, marking every 5cm with a marker so you can measure the rainfall.

Keep your gauge outside and when it's been raining, check to see how much water has fallen.

48 Mud castles

Squish and stack mud into a mound and add pebbles for decorations.

49 Boat race

When the rain stops, make paper boats to sail on puddles and even in the bath! Follow these instructions for a simple boat and see whose boat travels furthest.

You will need an adult's help.

BATH MAT

1 Fold an A4 sheet of paper in half.

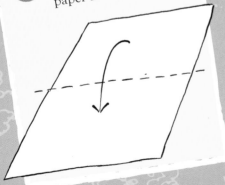

2 Fold corners to centre.

3 Fold bottom edges up – it looks like a paper hat.

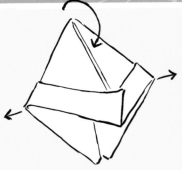

4 Pull apart the bottom edge and fold flat into a square shape.

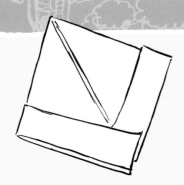

5 Tuck one flap under the other.

6 Fold up to create a triangle.

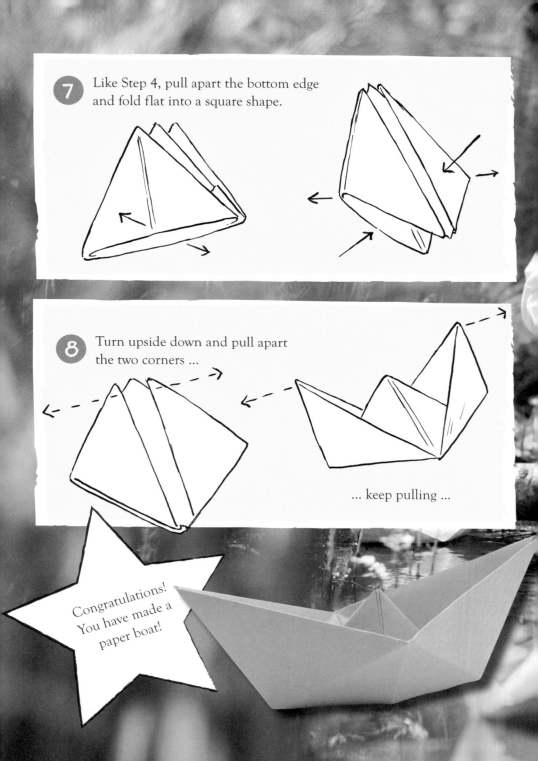

7 Like Step 4, pull apart the bottom edge and fold flat into a square shape.

8 Turn upside down and pull apart the two corners ...

... keep pulling ...

Congratulations! You have made a paper boat!

50 Library visit

'Would you read a Sustaining Book, such as would help and comfort a Wedged Bear in Great Tightness?'

On rainy days it's fun to go to the library to search the shelves for the perfect book – something new and exciting or an old favourite you cannot wait to read again.

You could also play at having a library at home with your own books!

How did you do?

Now you've tried lots of rainy day activities,
see which you enjoyed the most.

I was given this book by:

....

The most fun indoor activity was:

....

Something I tried for the first time was:

....

My favourite activity was:

....

Character cards

Cut these cards out to use in the book.

Pooh

Piglet

Tigger

Eeyore

Rabbit

Kanga

Roo

Christopher Robin

Gallery

Stick photos or draw pictures of your favourite activities here.

Index